Word Weavers
A First Anthology

Edited by Suzanne Power

Published in 2014
by Word Weavers Tramore
Co. Waterford, Ireland
www.facebook.com/wordweaverstramore

Cover photograph © Cecilia Carelse
Cover and interior designed by Cecilia Carelse

Printed by GK Print, Grannagh, Waterford

ISBN 978-0-9929274-0-0

Grant Aided by the Arts Office, Waterford Co. Council.

Waterford County Local Authorities
Údaráis Áitiúla Chontae Phort Láirge

Word n.
One of the units of speech or writing…

Weaver n.
To construct by combining separate elements
into a whole, to create…

ACKNOWLEDGEMENTS

Thanks to Margaret Organ, Arts Officer, Waterford County Council for support and advice on the anthology. We also gratefully acknowledge the support of Grant Aid from the Arts Office, Waterford County Council.

Thanks to Tracy McEneaney, for her encouragement, and all the staff in Tramore Library for their on-going support since the day Word Weavers was founded.

Thanks to Tramore Community Radio for providing a space for us to hold our meetings.

Thanks to Murph's Bar, Tramore, for sponsoring our launch and giving us a spot to write in during some of our summer excursions.

Thanks to our editor, Suzanne Power, for guiding us through the editing process to showcase our writing, and so much more.

A huge thanks to Cecilia Carelse because without her this book would still be a thought on the bookshelf of our minds.

Thanks to our families and friends.

Thanks to all Word Weavers members for their support and advice.

And finally, thanks to every writer in this anthology who found the courage to put their writing into print.

CONTENTS

FOREWORD

I would first of all like to acknowledge the courage of these writers in this Anthology to publically share their writing with us. To allow us a window into their innermost thoughts, characters, frustrations and creations.

To draw us into stories, perhaps of their imagination or maybe from an actual event or encounter which is marked in their memory and now is crafted by their words into these pages with short stories, prose and poems.

Writing by its nature is a solitary craft. Writers Groups can provide invaluable support to meet with like minded people, to receive feedback and support and to work together to a common purpose.

I hope that all the Word Weavers continue to weave words and that this publication may encourage those who are secretly scribbling to perhaps go to a writing workshop, or join a group so that the rest of us can enjoy the fruits of their labours.

Go n- éirí libh go léir.

Margaret Organ
Arts Officer/Oifigeach Ealaíon
Waterford County Council

INTRODUCTION

How are words woven?

No word exists merely on a page. When it is chosen, blended with time, experience, vision, clarity, reflection and imagination, it becomes the silver thread, the skein between life and the creative mind. Tapestries with words are not just to be observed, they are entered and lived, for authors, then for readers. They are dramatic acts, not flat renditions.

This is what the American short story writer Flannery O'Connor referred to as the textured environment. She learned to paint so she could improve her writing.

'...I have to write to discover what I am doing. Like the old lady, I don't know so well what I think until I see what I say; then I have to say it again.' She wrote in one of her letters.

'Strong emotions have much in common with each other and are timeless.' Contributor Bill Walsh says of his sonnet *Alice of Abervenny*.

The preceding quotes are true of every contributor to this book. Several of the writers in this anthology make the ancient past immediate. Their themes and descriptions are not just of the now, but ancient moments made now. Those writing in the present wove their themes, chose their contributions with care and with a sense of that contribution, that timelessness.

The words in this first anthology are more than play. They are polished, pearled and harmonised. Their writing represents not just a writers group gathering to share work in an Irish coastal town, but is an emblem of what heightened consciousness, combined artistic effort, can achieve. In a disposable culture, Word Weavers have created lasting impressions.

This accomplished book is a blend of textures in a carefully wrought story tapestry. Different threads, selected, combed, knotted, finding a unified achievement, inspiration you will remember. It gathers voices from all ranges, situations, sources and presents the reader with an opportunity to see their own shoreline, to walk their own story, while reading the poems and stories that comprise the first published testament of the Tramore based writers group Word Weavers.

Suzanne Power
Editor
2014

KATRIINA BENT

The Balcony
Out Of Focus
The Whistle Blow

The Balcony

You know that first moment between sleep and being awake? That precious moment before thoughts, anxieties or ideas start crowding in, robbing the peace and innocence of childhood, the warm, cosy, safe cocoon of the bed?

I know that so well. It's the only time of the day before the familiar pounding starts inside my head, the sequence and pace, the working of my mind gets more hectic, 'til I need to curl up in the corner of my room and just lie very still.

I'm not really sure what tipped the scales. It's like trying to pinpoint the high or low tide by the second, by an inch, by just watching from the shore. The isolation had grown on me so gradually that I was trapped in it before I knew it.

It was like adding paint on canvas, layer by layer, sometimes just a thin transparent wash. It formed a barrier that I was no longer able to cross.

There was a cut off point when the crammed existence indoors became the only reality I knew; camping inside my apartment stretched from weeks to months. I thought of people found dead in their apartments only when their neighbours were alerted to the stench.

It was early spring, mushy snow and grey skies. The last icicles dripping from the edge of the roof. I had a sense, almost a premonition, that things were about to change.

A simple revelation, but capable of sending my fried nerves into a chaos. The tiny crack in the well built walls and barriers caused a sudden and searing pain flash through my being.

I had tried to remove all causes of pain from my life with surgical precision. Now the harbinger of the unknown, penetrating into my obsessive order of things, was causing pain and I was unable to shelter myself from its advance.

I tried the usual; playing my music above all levels of

decibels, scratching and cutting myself 'til my flesh bled, even banging my head. Nothing seemed to help me to regain control of my self-created monotonous universe. Not this time.

Utterly exhausted, I fell asleep between the bed and the wall. Upon waking I knew someone was watching me. Feeling the familiar sensation of veins contracting and pulse racing, I waited. Someone or something was on the balcony.

I didn't dare to look, knowing that what I'd see would become an instrument of the change I dreaded. I didn't care if the starer burst through the door and killed me. In the end I had to take a weary glance.

On the balcony rail sat a small bird. It checked its surroundings, right eye slightly tilted forward, suspicious yet calm. Beyond it, the balconies of the apartment block across the way, a maze of concrete cubicles.

It tilted its head as if it had detected me, pressed its body low against the rail.

I started yelling like an animal and threw everything I could get my hands on at it, smashing the smallest glass panel on the balcony door.

The bird took flight. All I wanted was to grab it, squeeze it hard, and cut its head off.

After that experience, everything seemed to go out of sync. I couldn't stick to my routines. I felt unsafe, invaded, even violated. My inner world seemed to be losing its grip, coursing like an oil spill leaking out of a vehicle, dirty and damaging, showing its ugliness as it was seeping out. The outpour went on for days. I raged like the Gerasene demoniac.

On the ninth day, I woke up with a weird stillness within. A thought, pure and simple, came. I walked to get my laptop from the corner of the room where I'd thrown it. Browsing through a few sites I found pictures of small birds. I wanted to know what kind of bird had the astuteness to impinge on my life in such an infuriating way. Robin. A Robin. 'The European Robin', 'Erithacus rubecula', most commonly known in Anglophone Europe simply as the robin.

I could hear the dry voice of the professor lecturing on, stating these, and more facts, about this little passerine bird. Not a word was mentioned about encounters that worked like seismic seizures in the life and reality of a man.

In the end, I switched over to pictures of the little specimen and the more I stared the cloudier my vision became. I tried rubbing my eyes to clear them and felt the wetness on my face. I hadn't cried in years. I couldn't even if I had wanted to.

Tears now rushed down my face. This too seemed to go on for days. I was continually drawn out of myself and into increasing yearning to go onto the balcony. The fiery orange of the robin's chest probed the grey in my brain, pricking it, causing sore punctures, flashes of colour and emerging memories.

I stood behind the door, ran my hand over the shards of glass. Caressing the door handle. Until, one day I stepped out.

From then on, I spent increasing intervals on the balcony.

I washed my sheets, watered the remaining house plants that had survived the long drought. In fact I had tried to kill them as if that could put an end to the emptiness and longing caused by the leaving of my fiancée, sickened by my repeated refusal to go seek treatment.

I slowly began to experience the pleasant anticipation of opening the balcony door as my dulled and dying senses were rekindled by the world around that I'd been unable to connect with, although adjoined with it.

I knew that the time was nearing to unlatch the front door and walk again – hesitant steps in the bright light, more like a bat than a bird, blinking vigorously in order to see again.

Out Of Focus

There's a painting on the wall, one that she's seen countless times. It's an abstract, just a sketch really, one she's attempted to paint during times of remission. Those times seemed to grow ever shorter and relapses more frequent.

Yet, every once in a while, there was something she longed for; a moment of clarity. A time when colours, skies, people appeared wonderfully fresh, in harmony with each other and she felt a brief moment of belonging.

It wasn't one of those moments. The picture was a nauseating blur, her head shadowing and failing in essential connections. The diagnosis the doctor gave – bipolar disorder. It felt like a sentence passed, a life sentence, a stamp, a definition. She could recognise the 'disorder' part. Her interior world certainly was chaotic; fragments of clarity wrapped in anxiety and ancient fears. Over it all was a piece of tough, grey felt that occasionally lifted, letting in a shaft of light.

The 'bipolar' part she often wondered about. What were the two poles? They must resemble the two poles of the earth, one constantly in the light and the other plunged in perpetual darkness.

She somehow got it wrong in her navigations and had started gravitating towards the icy polar area with just the occasional flicker from the aurora. How did she get it so wrong? This question was always certain to lead her into fruitless despairing, circular thoughts heading nowhere.

This time, however, she had a growing sensation that it might turn out different. She made a decision to work through this day. To use what she had, to look kindly at her achievement.

Sitting on her bed, balancing herself, she focussed again on the painting. From the blur of colour, she suddenly traced the track in the undergrowth, under the sketchy flowers. How come she hadn't noticed it before? It appeared quite passable, even inviting. The path seemed to disappear into a hesitating glow of light into the horizon.

It was going to be a hard, long walk. There was no way she could pretend anything else. She would have to walk each day. Through the heavy days, the desperate days, the impossible days. The dull days. A long string of them.

She stood up, unsteadily, to go the bathroom. That would be the start.

The Whistle Blow

Several men had gathered around a small fire, smoking and smouldering more than giving off any real heat or light. Their shirts worn and faces telling a story of continued hardship. The oldest of them, a migrant worker like the rest, had brought some sausages and beer. The hissing sound of the fire, the smell of smoke mingling with the greasy aroma of the Krakow sausages.

After a few beers, he spoke up in Polish. He had left his native land without official documents, without a word of English and practically penniless. Things hadn't changed much since. He had grown older and wearier.

His wife had got tired of waiting and had taken off with a younger man, owner of a successful transport company, taking their two children with her.

This particular group of friends had become a replacement family for him.

The men were standing by a lake, along with other parties of foreigners, some fishing or camping overnight. The Irish found the lakes unpredictable and threatening, without the safe buoyancy of the sea. Russians, Polish, Estonians, and many others were drawn to them in search of homeland, the soft sweetness of the scented birches and lake water.

A Russian came from one of the other groups, introducing a large bottle of vodka. The bottle was passed around and as the night went on, they decided to throw off titles and clothing and headed for the lake.

It was one of those unusual and continental late summer nights. The lake had a narrow rim of shallow water and sand which turned into deep water without much of a warning. They were laughing and pushing each other around. The men were soon out of their depth but no one worried, they'd all learned to swim from an early age.

The old man enjoyed the soft currents of water against his body. He was still a strong swimmer with a good stride. He decided to head further out, towards the middle. Only a few feet away he kicked his legs and felt a searing pain in his right foot. He tried to move but knew instantly that his foot was tangled in something. He bent his upper body down and under and grasped the mesh of wire in his hands.

He suddenly remembered the countless times he had felt like letting go. Times when it felt that there was nothing left to hope for, when life was so gruesome that he'd allowed his mind to blend it into a blur with no distinct memories. Just a grey conveyor belt of events.

He let out a yelp. His mates were too far away, too drunk to hear him. They were loud, singing songs of communist times, interspersed with joking and laughter. He pulled at the mesh frantically. The water turned dark red in the moonlight. He kept struggling. A deep yearning within, an urge for survival swept thoughts of suicide, defeat, disillusion aside like a tidal wave.

Despite a growing weariness, he reached down and yanked his foot in a desperate effort to free it. He felt a loosening as the foot became disentangled with a piece of mesh still tied around the ankle. He turned on his back to save his strength. Being in water, he didn't know how much blood he was losing but from the dizziness and a high pitched whistle in his ears, he knew that it was a lot and he had to reach the shore and his peers.

He was finally spotted by the Russian with the now empty bottle, who lunged into the water, grabbing the old man, pulling him to the shoreline, banging him between the shoulder blades, ripping off his own shirt between strikes, to make a strap for the bleeding.

Another man was fumbling for his mobile, trying to dial an emergency call. The old man wept. Everyone thought it was the pain and shock, but he knew they were tears of joy, strong tears of life, bursting through once more.

CECILIA CARELSE

Cecilia Carelse

Floating With Crocodiles

Time ends here.
Slope and deluge,
then silence under water.

I float, waiting.
Dark shapes move in the murky gloom.
Black sky above the surface.

Suspended in flux.
Preparing for them to strike.
They come close enough for me to feel the hard skin knock.
The swish of a tail.

But it's the charge that frightens me the most.
That moment of attack when their jaws will catch me,
hold me tight,
drag me under and away from this place,
to turn me over and over until I lie limp and dying.

All these fears run through my mind
in the world below the surface,
while I float
and wait
for them to come.

Are You Ready To Let Her Go?

I see the pain in your eyes.
I see you fight with sorrow.
Inner turmoils, bound together.
No release screams the heart.

I see your lips shake.
I see you hold back the anguish.
Sounds and words push to be heard.
All gone, crushed in breath.

I see your hands tremble.
I see them tighten the sodden tissue.
If only to grab hold,
To touch her, be near, once more.

I see your tears fall.
I see your body catch waves of grief.
No words can stop the pain.
It flows on, years to follow.

I want to say
all will be well
but it won't.
Yesterday, you lost your mother.
Today, you buried her.
Nothing will be the same again.

Ironing

The old ironing board.
My strongest supporter.
I let the music flow and
press clothes with love
into flattened fabric below.

I could give it away.
Be gone to a charity shop,
up there, in the window,
antique on display
or local treasures museum.

But it's my laundry storage
brought in out of
the damp conservatory,
clothes left lying in layers,
until its sight I bear no more.

The NOW CD's are by choice
and I dance before its altar
as I flip, fold, press, preen,
aspire to elegance
in my creased life.

That Fine Line

I run that fine line
between almost normal conversation
with you, and
saying something wrong,
inappropriate.
I cannot predict
words that you don't like to hear,
don't want to hear.
Words that will offend you,
my vaguest ideas.

Listen and wait,
for the change in tone of your voice,
to annoyance, to anger,
to short phrases designed
to subdue my voice
and regain control of me.

Your prejudice, he says,
you always challenge me.
Slices through my heart,
into guilt
carved with years of fear,
through childhood,
of opening my mouth,
revealing my thoughts,
or even the barest opinion,
contradictory only to him.

I must stand apart,
regain my pride, my own strength,
but never 'challenge'.

Cecilia Carelse

Oh, that is the word.
He considers it a challenge to him,
to his authority as man of his house,
dictated to him by the fiction of his religion,
and by customs allowed an African man.

I call it just talking,
a discussion,
but keep quiet,
say nothing,
shut my mouth, again.
Hope to appease the silent rage
surrounding my physical being,
or across the miles of space between us,
in the afterwards of a phone call cut short.

So I tiptoe every conversation,
(they are not arguments
as he wants to call them)
gently, cautiously,
listen only to him speaking,
never reveal my own life.
So that, as Mum calls it,
we can keep the peace.

They Asked Me To Write About God

They asked me to write about God.
Thought about it.
I said,
probably not.
Without faith
what is there
when else-wise is my belief.

Politely put,
I don't
believe in
fairies,
tales
or history.
Because I know
even my own memoirs
do not reflect truly
what happened.

The Blue Woman

The hurt and curl
is cut into her nude.
Blue calm, cold, contained.
Angular edges under lies.
Head bend low to hide
from inquisition fears.
The frozen woman, on the floor.
Exposed, alone.

Almost cruel to keep you here,
my pet.
There you are.
Are you ready?
Then unravel and stand.
Your time is now.
Come along.
Come along with me.

Leaving Home

You leave home, this morning, and decide that today is the day and there is no going back. You place the milk bottles out on the front door step, turned the right way out in the wire basket. Lock the front door behind you and the wind catches your scarf. You retie it as you trace your way towards the bus stop.

You wait but deep inside you are scared, of being seen here at this time of day, at this place. But you reassure yourself that he's nowhere near here, he's at work, he can't see you, and it's all in your mind.

You didn't take much with you. Your purse and a shopping bag, in case. And the roll of money you have been saving for this very day, and your passport. You want nothing from that house; you have served a life inside it, for him and the one before who made him. As soon as you can, you will buy new clothes and discard what you are wearing.

You look up the street for the bus and curse. When it comes, it will take you from here to the town centre, to the train station, to the boat, to another country.

As you wait, you question yourself until you change your mind and eventually, like yesterday morning, and every day before that, you turn around and go home again.

You know tomorrow is the day you will leave him and promise yourself that it will happen. You get back inside the house, remove the scarf, stash away the money safely, and begin the daily process to ensure that everything in the house is ready for him, your son, when he comes home tonight.

Cecilia Carelse

Trapped

The relief was instant. Johnny reached for the bog roll and pulled out a huge wad around his fist. Time to make shapes out of this tiny cubicle, now the pressure was off. Besides, there was a fine young one gyrating at the karaoke that he'd his eye on.

The only stick in his plan this evening, was the dodgy leftover Chinese he'd found in with the empty drink cans in the kitchen. Couldn't be sure when he'd got it home. Looked untouched and hunger had him by the gut so he'd stuffed his face with it this afternoon for breakfast. Four hours later, and four large shots of crème de menthe, the only bottle with alcohol left in the flat, how it got there was any man's guess, and the five Guinness on top of that lot by the time he'd got to Mattie's pub, and the heavens had opened up down below, so to speak.

Job done, he grabbed his jeans up from his ankles.

'Oh, fuck,' he cursed out loud, the words reverberating through the two stalls in the men's. Some eejit had wet the tiles below the bowl and, in the speed needed to get his arse on the porcelain, he'd ignored the state of the floor. The wet patch was only the size of a navvies hand but he couldn't walk out with that between his legs. He'd have to stand under the dryer to sort it. Didn't smell much like piss from here but the mucky bit was already suctioning itself to the skin at his groin.

He was fixing the jeans buckle when he heard the outer door slam open.

'I'll have yer money,' a man said, 'no need for all dis show.'

'I don't give a fuck about that. I know you're good for it. You tell me where that dickhead Johnny Boy is. I swear I saw him in here. If he's after fucking off, you're gonna get it tonight.'

'Ah Declan, it's not like that. I don't know the man.'

'What you calling me? Call me Deccie. I hate that name.'

Johnny swore under his breath. It was Fat Declan putting

the bollocks on, and he was only guessing this, Patsy Connor. Jeez, Fat Declan was fair thick, your typical loaded Mammy's boy from the Southside. Patsy only lived in the flat opposite Johnny, wasn't even his friend. Never had anything to do with that old man. Surely, a pensioner by now. Never saw him at the social, unless he was the lucky over-fifties that didn't need to sign on but once a year. Never saw anyone leave that man's flat either.

A fist pounded the door of his cubical.

'Get the fuck out.' It was Fat Declan. 'Or I'll be coming in.'

Behind the door, Johnny let off a low groan. Well, he'd been feeling that way a few minutes ago. He made the shittiest, sick sound he could.

'Can't move. Urrrgh,' he said. Then he put the two fingers down his throat, unloaded black and then green filth, into the toilet. That'd stop the man.

'Ah, jeez,' Fat Declan howled on the other side of the door. Johnny let off a wild moan.

'Find him,' Fat Declan shouted, 'don't you leave until you tell me where he is.'

'Yeah, yeah,' Patsy said, 'I'll find him for yer.'

'I'm getting out. The smell in here.'

The outer door banged again. Johnny pinched his nose but the reek of his own vomit came into his mouth and made him want to throw some more.

'He's gone,' Patsy called out. 'D'yer hear me, Johnny?'

Johnny held his breath. Put a hand on the door as if to separate him from what'd be coming on the other side.

'I know yer came in here. Saw yer run like der bull was on your tail. I didn't tell him where yer are. No business of mine. Don't know why he thinks I know yer.'

Johnny flushed the toilet, unlocked, and pulled open the cubicle door.

'Jeez.' Patsy gave a whistle. 'Yer look a shit.'

Johnny moved past him to the one sink and rinsed his

mouth out. He put his hands under the air dryer, tilting his hip forward for the wet patch to catch some of the action.

'Thanks for saying nothin',' he said to Patsy. 'I owe yer.'

'Ah, yer ok. Look Johnny, yer a young man, what yer, thirty? Well, yer can't go on like this. Sort yourself out. How much yer owe der man?'

'Seven hundred.'

Patsy pulled a bunch of fifties from his pocket.

'Ders the seven. I'll give Declan the money. You're paid off then. Yeah?'

Johnny nodded like a dozy dog.

'I can't take your money,' he said. Was a lie but he was relieved by the gesture.

'Ah, no worries. Consider it done,' Patsy said. 'Now yer owe me. Ok?'

'Ok.'

'Right so.'

Patsy pulled out the door.

The squawks of someone's granny belted into the sour air around Johnny.

Patsy paused, turned to him, and gave a sly wink.

'Good thing's I know where yer live. There'll be no trouble. I'll get my money back. Alrigh'? Yeah?'

GEORGE WILLIAM CURRAN

The Free Spirit
Childhood's End
Looking To Know
Is It True That Thou Art Love?
The Butterfly
I Wish I Were A Grain Of Sand
Lakeside Reflection
Melted Wax
Now And Then I Think Of You
The Tree Of Thought
My Sweet Sister Melancholy

The Free Spirit

I am a free spirit,
In freedom I fly.
Knowing no limit,
In an infinite sky.
In a sky ever changing,
Ever changing am I.
Every day learning,
New ways to fly.

Childhood's End

Thinking now of this weary life,
Remembering then the peace of childhood.
Upon my face the smile of morn,
Wanting now, things unknown then.

Looking To Know

I
Not knowing
Went looking
Not looking
Found knowing
I know now not to look
But know not where

Is It True That Thou Art Love?

Is it true that thou art love and I am truth?
That thou art all, as I am endless?
Being endless, not knowing where,
Knowing only in truth, that thou art there.

The Butterfly

I held a butterfly in my hand,
From its flight it took its rest,
This little creature of sky and land.
I held it to my breast.
There for a time it was mine,
But how soon I did forget,
How this little spark of sunshine
On release would bring regret.

I Wish I Were A Grain Of Sand

I wish I were a grain of sand
Time at sea, time on land,
Existence but a beach of dream,
In my sanded shadow realm.

Tide my time, world my place,
Being, but my only fate,
Stars above, sand on beach,
Infinity never far from reach.

World within, a world apart,
Piece of stone, without a heart,
Piece of stone spared by pain,
Untouched by tears, a hardened grain.

No love to take, no love to give,
My only dance a tidal jig,
Existence but as though a dream,
The gull of the sea my only scream.

No thoughts of today, nor tomorrow,
Untouched by taint of human sorrow
No thoughts of my grains nearby,
Do they laugh, or do they cry.

Never anger or aggression,
nor the burden of possession,
no loss, no fear, no pride of place,
just a tiny grain without a face.

Never the need to seek a mate,
Nor thought to war, thought to hate,
Just timeless tide and endless sand,
To be a grain, that were grand.

Lakeside Reflection
(Dedicated to Lara)

Lakeside reflection who art thou?
Appearing as my head did bow,
Did I from nothing your image create?
That my countenance does imitate.

On the surface floats my face,
Moving amidst the water's grace,
You are an image, you are not real.
But my reflection you did steal.

Reflection and water one in kind,
I see you, but you are blind,
Understanding evades your depth,
You have never laughed or wept.

I am real, but you are not,
An illusion temporal, soon forgot.
A mirage of sorts nothing more,
The water being a reflective door.

By a stroke of the hand, you melt away.
You are gone, but here I stay,
Perhaps too, to reflect another's face,
On a faraway lakeside, in a faraway place.

Melted Wax

A –
Blank page –
No longer –
Blank.
A candle –
Alight.
My mind –
Flows –
Ink –
The medium.
That world –
My world –
Liquid thoughts –
To –
Hardened words.
Solidifying –
On –
Paper –
Like –
Melted wax.

Now And Then I Think Of You

Now and then
I think of you,
Someone long long ago
Whom I once knew.

Far, far away,
In time,
In place,
How I'd love to see your face.

To see you smile,
To hear you speak,
To wipe the tears
From my cheek.

Thinking of
The times we had,
The sunny days
They make me glad.

Where are you now?
I do not know.
Are you happy?
I hope so.

I am happy
I suppose,
My happiness temporal
Like the summer rose.

But a happiness less fragile,
If only I knew
You now think of me
As I think of you.

The Tree Of Thought

How beautiful a sensation is thought,
Like a tree it grows and weaves
In it men have climbed and sought,
Answers from its flowers and leaves.

In its branches tempests quiet.
They have worn and wisdom brought,
Out from darkness, shade and light,
That we might think, what they have thought.

Thoughts which are in tree the root.
Source from which the mind is fed.
Reflection, contemplation, the growing shoot,
As into insight, and knowing we are led.

Then from bud, fruit of shape,
Of which is seed of thought anew.
In time, it other thoughts will make,
In other trees like me and you.

My Sweet Sister Melancholy

You come sometimes in autumn
The falling leaves your heartbeat
Quickening my pulse
In colours of black and grey
When you are almost forgotten
I see you in a picture
Hear you in a piece of music
I recognise you in a stranger's face
I feel you as rain
I walk to you always
I return your dark smile
Always your slave
My sweet sister melancholy
Ever changing, ever the same
I know you
I fear you. I long for you
You are a moon
I am a tide
Where do you go?
Why do you return?
What gift have you brought?
I give myself a gift to you
Stay awhile then leave
I will await your return
And if you do not
I will mourn your passing.

BILLY FENTON

Ripples

A single drop from a grey sky,
Hits still water,
Ripples are born.

Another drop falls,
Another circular world is born,
Expands.

Before long, the pond is covered,
In watery growths,
Turbulence begins.

Circles meet circles,
Ripples displace ripples,
Like lovers and haters in play.

The drops stop,
The sky clears,
Calmness resumes.

Ag Fás

Little child,
Man in black,
Life destroyed.

Little children,
All bad, they're told.
Lives set back.

Adults now,
Still unsure,
Lives on hold.

Badness disguised as goodness,
Fooled us, lost us,
Disabled us.

Blue

Jonas drifts out of sleep. Rather than the damp cold he is used to, his left cheek tingles with an unfamiliar warmth. When he opens his eyes, he jumps in fright. A beam of light across his pillow, growing outward from a hole in the boarded-up window, a million particles of dust floating across it. He considers it fearfully, and his concern moves slowly towards curiosity. What is it, where is it coming from? His eyes following it from the bed to the window and back. Slowly, he reaches out, his hand disturbing it; the shadow of his fingers growing over the pillow. He plays with it, in and out, up and down, warm, cold, his smile growing. Outside, he hears voices, excited voices.

'Jonas, come quick, you must see this.' It is Mother's voice from the bottom of the stairs.

Everyone is on the street. They are looking up, pointing, laughing, their faces immersed in it. A break in the clouds; a deep blue; a circle of yellow that pushes Jonas to look away, but he can't, even though it hurts him.

'It's the sun, the sun.'

'I thought I would never see it again.'

'He is no longer angry for what we have done.'

'The sky is so blue, so beautiful.'

'It feels so good on my face.'

'They said it would be another hundred years. They were wrong, just like they were last time.'

Mother hugs Jonas tightly.

Just like the pictures in my school books, he thinks, only so much better.

Blue continues to grow. Birds, normally silent, remember their music, their bodies shooting back and forth across it. The black water dancing over the collapsed bridge shimmers with rainbow light. Dead green starts to live, starts to shine, starts to glisten. Faces, normally dour, radiate.

For three hours the world is a different place, the kind of place that the old people speak about, before the Earth closed in on human greed.

Then it begins to shrink, and blue turns back to grey. They wait, but only thick clouds remain. Bodies sunken with grief turn towards home. The birds continue to fly but do not sing. The river is lifeless again. And a single tear floats down Jonas' face.

'If it came back once, it will come back again, Jonas,' Mother says.

'When will it come back, when will we see the sky again?' he asks.

'Soon,' she says.

'You do not know, Mother, do you?'

As she holds him tightly, a tiny gap, only a hair's breadth wide, opens above them. A tiny sliver of blue. Then it is gone.

'Did you see that?' Jonas says.

'Yes, it came back, Son.'

'It came back, so it can come back again.'

'Yes, it will come back again.'

A Summer Shower

Jack Devere rests easily in the deck chair, the folds of his flesh sagging through the gaps, his brow glistening, his fingers tapping to music from a secret world. Nearby his wife Dora sits on the sand, building a fairy tale world for their youngest Kate.

'This is the tower,' Dora says. 'Like the one Rapunzel lived in.'

'Can I use this for a window?' Kate says holding up a flat stone.

'Yes, that's perfect lovey. You put it where you want.'

A short distance away, their son Jack Junior digs his pelvis into the sand, its warmth scraping against his back and legs. Every so often he scans the beach. Nora Casey, a girl from his school, is changing into her swimming gear. She smiles at him, drops the side of her towel for a second so he can glimpse the roundness of her breast. He feels himself blush and he turns quickly and pretends to watch a dog that is chasing a ball. When he looks back she is walking in his direction, her body swaying, her hand playing with her hair, her red swimsuit shining.

Then she stops, looks at him directly and points towards the sea. He moves his body slightly and watches her running towards the water. Slowly he stands, looks at his father, and follows her.

A pellet of rain bounces off Devere's cheek, a warm nasty thing. He twitches, opens his eyes, a mottled black is eating into the sun. Two more drops hit him like a blade cutting into his heart. He pushes himself upright.

'What kind of a country is this? Never a moment's fucking peace. Where are you going?' He shouts at Jack Junior.

More drops fall like a machine gun warming up.

Dora stands, looks at the sky and scoops Kate into her arms.

Then the sky lets loose, like someone is piercing the skin which is holding Sunday together. Everyone races for the car park, taking with them whatever they can carry. The beach drains like a swarm of bees returning to a hive, their voices competing to outdo the sound of the rain.

'Isn't it great I won't need a shower later.'

'I'm moving to Spain, enough of this.'

'I'm for Brady's; a nice cool cider.'

'Will they ever get the forecast right?'

'Sure isn't it better than snow?'

Jack Devere slams the car door shut. He pushes his hands through his hair, shakes them, the drops spattering the dash board.

'One day of the week for a bit of peace and what happens? What happens? What fucking happens?' He searches through his pockets. 'Where's my cigarettes? Don't tell me.' He glares at Dora. He looks in the rear view mirror.

Jack Junior is sitting upright his head bowed.

'You go get them.'

'Can't it wait until…' Dora says.

'Go - get them.'

Kate starts to cry.

Jack Junior runs across the beach, now deserted, but strewn with the colours of summer. The rain pours over him, down his neck and back. He feels the sand squelch under his feet as he runs. Where were we sitting? He looks around, sees a dissolving castle of sand, races in that direction. There's his deck chair. He looks around, sees the box on the ground and picks it up, and runs as quickly as he can back to the car.

'Are you OK, Junior?' his mother asks.

'Of course, he's OK.' Devere grabs the box, and it collapses in his fist. He opens his hand, stares at it in disbelief, turns and looks at Junior, his blue eyes turning to fire, his skin trembling, his lips twitching, his body restless, but trapped by the rain.

'Jesus, can't you be more careful. When I get you home.'

'It's not his...' Dora whispers.

'Shut up.'

Devere opens the window, reaches out, closes his fist, and cardboard mush oozing brown drains to the ground. He reaches for the ignition, the engine screeches to life, and the car lurches into the car park.

'The rain will stop in a minute,' Dora says. 'It's only a summer shower.'

Devere glares at her.

'Mammy, are we going home?' Kate asks quietly, her head now buried deep in Dora's chest.

'Yes, lovey. We can play…'

'Shut up.'

Jack Junior pulls the window down, just enough so he can see through the crack. He is looking for a silver Mazda 6. At the end of the car park he sees it, and through its back window, he finds the red colour he has been looking for, the tanned flesh, the black hair. The roadside turns to a fuzzy green as the car accelerates. Through the rear window he watches the other cars blur into the distance. Doors are opening as people emerge back into the sunshine.

The red of Nora's swimsuit moves across the silver of the Mazda. He turns and stares at the back of his father's head, his blue eyes burning with anger, his body shaking, his lips mouthing words he dare not speak. His mother is staring straight ahead, Kate is sobbing quietly, the radio comes on, loudly, one of those operatic arias that he hates. Through the rear window the car park can no longer be seen, the sea sparkles with a million diamonds, the sky screams with a summer blue.

Then he opens the car door and he jumps.

DARA FOLEY

And Cherry Blossom Watches Over Samurai In Equal Measure
Island Shores
The Interceding Calm
The Noumena
Transience
Innocence; Revisited
Rin Gong
Vancouver

And Cherry Blossom
Watches Over Samurai
In Equal Measure

Double sided Japanese flags as subtle a message as Pearl Harbour.
The humble natives exact nobility from their ancient sunrise;
Gai-Jin subconscious warding.

Long and age-old strategists, the finest minds of Middle Ages
- when such began to matter.
They wrote the book
The strategy of art.
Some others too.

They knew to train the mind to finest point,
Those artisans of patience, and dexterity.
They innovated tiered society
And never tore it down.

They knew to use a beachhead for the trappings of their trade,
The safety net yet safer with a western balustrade.
They understand the need for free release, and lost potential;
They understand untouchable and intimate perfection.

The Geisha. The Samurai.
Swordplay and words;
The elegance of self-effacement;
Hidden inner lords.

Dara Foley

Island Shores

The purple pink and green surprise
To grass and heathers, sun, I rise
The blue the trees the hanging lines
The flagpoles, people, sails, and lies

I trust the birds in seven step
So small the log not broken yet
The islands and the trees survive
The breeze and water - most alive

With thoughts and dreams of years to spend
To sing and write and never end
The people come and go and may
Surprise the night by finding day

Among the waterways and stones
The beaches and the righteous thrones
We find our own insipid ways
And mildly pass a simple haze

The student with the epic loans
The loner with the hardened bones
The energetic simple mind
The turbine chugs along behind

Our destination tried and true
Vancouver Island, oh so blue
I throw away my last resorts
And time has come for fresher starts

The Interceding Calm

Among the flies
The sparrow soars
Agency within

Seated silence
Clatters keys.

Insipid spirals
While the software laughs;
Soaking in the errors,
Sidelong glances,
And telephones

A mindful clarity emerges
From the office of the damned

A rubberised cacophony
Multiply excitedly
While the eyes compose the world

The Noumena

Sparks
Arcing off the welder's floor
Herein the god particle's abundance
Creator's torch and mask

Inception moulding thoughts and steel
At once
At last
At ease

Creation in the first degree
Creator's sculpted hands
Primed

We try to show each other perfect ideas
From our perfect mindscapes
In our perfect minds

We spend the time

In tedium we
toiling with imperfect forms;
Intending to craft a wholesome part
of our intention, to give at least inception
of a thread of thought that might in some
way - in someone else's perfect mindscape
Approach the inimitable beautiful perfection
of The Thing That Cannot Be

The perfect new idea from an isolated perfect world

But there are three parts to be self conscious of
And few can master all regards of these;
Many fail by only factoring in validity, originality and excellence,
Many forget the translation to the mortal realm,
And more forget the presentation

Some just copy the Creators, and do much better for it
As the Creators have already trained us
to accept their translations and presentations
And we were made to be trained

Sparks
Arcing off the welder's floor

Transience

I'll make you fly away with me embracing debonair
I'll take us to the shadows of the moon upon the air;
We'll monitor the blue, the green, the lizard in the tree
The sandy curve of coconuts and specious dignity

The island of the moonlit fires
The rapture and the light;
The climbing of the waterfalls
The falling of the night

The list of things I think about
Intentions muddy will;
And even in the modern life
I cannot find my fill

The passion in a nature walk
The forest for the trees;
The lighting and the motive cars
But specks upon the breeze

The simplest little cove reminds
Ideas old instilled;
That freedom is abundant fruit,
But fruit we cannot build

Innocence; Revisited

Twilight Fires that dance with life itself;
These eyes were made to smile.

The smile of an angel
And instantly my soul is calm;
We two of caution and subtle intricacy
Relax, and let our thoughts laugh loud.
The humour in your tone and timbre marks a wisdom
I never thought to find.

I remember being content to hold and feel the feeling grow;
I remember our flamenco and our pas de deux.
You make me feel like a natural,
Like before the fall of innocence.

Our eyes intertwine,
And for once I ask an open question:

May I have this dance?

Rin Gong

Two hours late
The turbulent wind spits wispy wet snow
Stopping only for the glasses

Stopping only for the coffee
To enjoy the saltless air
The ivy poison tree visages
Shotgun meditation.

Those snapshot moments of nothingness
Cohesion captured vividly until Athena rides again;
Rides again - into war

The subject hasn't changed, not substantively
Just another layer of abstracted misdirection
Leading you lovingly down the garden path

My garden path.
Yes I've walked it and taken nothing in
Nothing ever in, for good, for bad

But wispy wet snow boils my blood
And fires my spirit to new heights
Reminding frosted cities to stay crisp in my mind
Reminding me to fly between the tallest buildings
Open heart in open hand

Tibetan Rhythms and new seasons;
The Schrodinger Paralysis.

Sometimes,
Snowflakes never touch the ground

Dara Foley

Vancouver

As dawn encapsulates the night
And clouds escape the still
The feathers and the moon combine
To oversee the hill

The slopes are white and trees are bare
And barren rules the will
The reddest shaft of light decides
The conifers to fill

The valley full of winding tree
The trickle over dam
The peaceful interrogative
Salu salaam salaam

As darkness lifts the beauty mask with unintending skill
I contemplate the morning light,
The parachute,
The thrill

LYNDA GOUGH

Sisters
Sandhills
The Grand Aunt (Annie Dohnáll Bán)
Birdboy
Clonycavan Man (Bog Body Circa 300 B.C.)
Wild Words
For Seamus

Sisters

We shared the same womb.
Heard the same sounds
a heartbeat from above.

Swam in the same amniotic fluid.
Built our separate umbilical cords.
Pushed our life down the same canal.

We shared the same room.
Heard the same sounds.
Late night telly through lino.

Swam in early morning waters.
Built our separate chlorinated dreams.
Pushed our way down sided lanes.

We shared the same tomb.
Heard the same sounds.
His heartbeat stopped.

Swam in the same flood.
Built our separate ways through loss.
Pushed our way down grief's canal.

Sandhills

When they broke,
he broke.
Crumbled to fragments,
no former self.

His life memories,
full speed.
Reeled on uncertain
wheels.

Early morning stomps,
their dog.
Undulating sandhills,
his refuge.

Shouting at shifting sand,
cursing, regretting.
It drank the whys?
Infinite what ifs.

Cold mornings turned,
short sleeves.
Monotonous grey broke
to African swallows.

His turmoil lifted,
skyward.
Carried his questions
away.

The Grand Aunt (Annie Dohnáll Bán)

Cataracts hide the blue.
Crystal tears hardened.

No sliver of light now.
Lids that back on to blackness.

Images of the sea.
Footage fades in memory.

Her ears more alert now.
Catch cockles shifting in shells.

Children soft toe around her.
Tiny breaths held tight.

Wide nostrils catch them.
Her mind's sight, grab small hands.

Her baby mouth, toothless.
Gaping lips, sucks salt.

Squirming fingers fill her tongue.
Two darkened eyes release the sea.

Birdboy

Locked up on Spike Island at 16 yrs.
The birdboy fell.
Drunk on double bumblers.
Sweet cider held him down.

First of life's fruitless shocks.
All colour went.
Followed by his every hair.
His growth of manhood frozen.

Twelve months brought his release.
To incarcerated freedom flew.
Built bird boxes in the coalhouse.

Cocooned in canary yellow,
Birdboy honed his avian skills.
Incubated plumage, hatched porcelain eggs.
The coalhouse lost its blackness.

Birdboy never flew from home.
Drank sweet cider beside his mother.
Who incarcerated herself for 20 yrs.
While her agoraphobic jailer dangled the key

Clonycavan Man (Bog Body Circa 300 B.C.)

And they left their axes fall.
And three times they hit my head.
And pine resin shattered with my skull.
And spilled my stomach seed and milk.
And brown bog soaked my blood.
And they sliced my kingly nipples.
And all submissive suckling stopped.
And kestrels cried to drown my screams.
And soft lichen scratched my eyes.
And lady land was satisfied.
And cut in two they laid me bare.
And offered her my twisted hand.
And she took it in her greedy rasp.
And drank me in her deep waters.
And years laid upon years.
And men hunting for heat found me.
And gazed upon my leathered skin.
And saw their eyes in mine.

Wild Words

I pressgang words.
Coerce, corral, collect.

Forge the iron stanza.
Shape its beauty to fit.

Wrap its scorching arc.
To reluctant hooves.

Nail home each comma.
Full trot, no stop.

Watch it rear and kick.
Its stubborn eye seared.

Dip it in cold truth.
Steam, sooth its hurt.

Heeled four-fold.
Set to run the risk.

Wild, untamed, carefree.
Words unleashed.

For Seamus

Seamus, you will never know
how I flattened your collection.
Burst your spine, heard it creak.
How I crushed your every sinew.

Seamus, you will never know
How I forced our copulation.
Laid my barren pages
against your fertile words.

Seamus, you will never know
how when I saw you I could not speak.
Stolen words caught my throat.
How I longed to tell you
you had fathered a poet.

ROSALINE MURPHY

Homage To Hathor
The Shopping Centre
The Sacrificed Child
Light And Dark
Lust For Life
The Silent Grandmother
Lost
The Vessel

Homage To Hathor

Cool clean white-washed walls
Creating a place of sanctity, a place of holiness.
A place of quiet silence that slowly envelops and embraces
With one step across the threshold.
A place for separating, blending, stirring, churning, patting.
A place of waiting, a place of alchemy.
Where fresh, foaming fluids are transformed
Into sun coloured bars of gold
A true and humble temple of Hathor and her rich gifts to
mankind
A glass of milk, a slice of cheese, a simple pat of butter.

Rosaline Murphy

The Shopping Centre

The edifice rises,
Vast
In its construction.
Marble slabs
Loom,
Above
An entrance,
Imposing
In its grandeur.
I enter,
Awestruck.

Floating music,
Whispers
Welcome.
Expectancy
Hovers
A flashing thought,

Humanity's new
Religion
And
This,
Its home,
Its Temple.

The Sacrificed Child

Alone am I
In a world of nothingness

Let them beat the drum
Let them beat the drum
'Til the answers come
'Til the answers come

An eternity ago
I spoke much
I heard much
Now…

Let them beat the drum
Let them beat the drum
'Til the answers come
'Til the answers come

I have long ceased to look upon
The world that lies at my feet
The world that
Abandoned me
Left me
Sacrificed me
To this lonely perch

Let them beat the drum
Let them beat the drum
'Til the answers come
'Til the answers come

How long has passed since…
I care not

Let them beat the drum
Let them beat the drum
'Til the answers come
'Til the answers come

An eternity of
Glimpses, scraps of memory
That tortured,
Haunted
Taunted
Passed
Then…
No more

Let them beat the drum
Let them beat the drum
'Til the answers come
'Til the answers come

Give them our prayers,
They said,
The elders said
The people said
Parents said
Father…Mother…said

Let them beat the drum
Let them beat the drum
'Til the answers come
'Til the answers come

They never came…they never came

The people left…still waiting
The village died…still waiting
I alone remain
No longer waiting
For gods that never came
For gods that will never come.

Let them beat the drum
Let them beat the drum
For gods that will never come
For gods that will never come

Five thousand years, they said
The people said,
I waited.
For gods to come,

But people came
Villagers came
Someone else's mother came
And took me from the mountain

Let them beat the drum
Let them beat the drum
'Til the answers come
'Til the answers come

Five thousand years
The answer has come
The answer has come
Ye are the gods
Ye are the gods

Still they do not see
Still they look for answers
Answers that will never come
Until they choose to see

For I am the Sacrificed Child,
And the people wait, the elders wait
For the answer that now stands before them

Let them beat the drum
Let them beat the drum
'Til the answers come
'Til the answers come

But they do not see
They do not hear
That Ye are the Gods
Ye are the Gods
That you have been waiting for.

Light And Dark

Prisms of light burst forth, reaching out into the darkness, seeking to devour the very night itself. Entranced, we watch the fires flame, the light of the sun, moon and stars. We gaze at dazzling sunlight dancing on the sea's surface. We are fascinated by the sparkle of gemstones, the stars of films and reality shows, the colour on our television screens, laptops and phones. The dance of light and shadow.

What are we searching for?

Do our eyes betray us when we look at the shimmering things?
Are we so bedazzled that we no longer recognize the beauty and treasure that exists in the dark, like little seeds in the womb of the world waiting to be born?
Are we so blinded by the glitter that surrounds us that we no longer seek the Pearl of Great Price that lies within each of us waiting to be discovered and embraced?

Galileo said that the greatest jewel in the world is the earth with which we are clothed.

What a beautiful thought, to be able to truly see, that each person we meet is a jewel of the earth, and within that earth there is an even greater jewel, the Pearl of Great Price: the inner light that dwells within us all. The wisdom of the soul. The greatest gift of all.

Lust For Life

An ocean of sadness, lies before me
Filled with the tears of the world.
Tears shed by countless eyes that once
Gleamed with light and the lustful yearnings of life
Now cried out into the oceans' depths

The gloom laden clouds part
Pale pillars of light break through
Searching the waters below
Water droplets feeling the glimmer of heat
Leap into the light, and are drawn back into the sky.
A new cycle of lust for life begins

Rosaline Murphy

The Silent Grandmother

About eighty, almost invisible, always dressed in black, always silent. Her only companion, her rosary beads.

If beads could speak what story would they reveal? Of her thoughts, her hopes, her dreams, her silent and secret self poured into those beads. Were they a true companion? Did they serve her well, I wonder? What would her life have been without them? Was she richer or poorer for them?

I salute my grandmother. How can I not, I would not be here without her. I salute her and I value her and I honour her.

I have no hugs or kisses of little conversations to remember her by. Did I lack something by not receiving these little signs of love and affection? No, how can I miss what was never there. Is that not false imagining? Did that mean she lacked love, my silent black garbed Grandmother? I think not.

I write this to give witness to Her, to all grandmothers like her, who struggled and strived to bring up their children as best they could. Who, when husbands died, deserted them or turned to drink, were abandoned, to ponder, to dream, to desire, alone. And so they turned to their rosaries. Their one source of strength that could never be taken from them and that helped them survive.

My grandmother's outer self was like a husk: dried and withered and seemingly lifeless. But her inner self was beautiful, vibrant, alive. Yes, I might have no hug or secret word or little sign of affection to remember her by, but what I do have is a gift, more precious, stronger than anything I could have wished for.

Her gift to me – a simple faith, a lighted torch that might be invisible to the eyes of the world but to me and to all who chose to look beyond the visible, her legacy to me is that lighted torch of faith that will see me safely through this world and beyond.

And for this, I thank and honour my Silent Grandmother.

Lost

The white ribbon that held his pyjama bottoms in place protruded from beneath his jumper. This image of himself slowly leaked its way into his brain, surprising him with its innocence, its normality. He paused, watching his reflection. He didn't know what was wrong with him today. He felt out of sorts and it was more than needing his first drink of the day. He leant forward, clutching the wash hand basin with his two hands, feeling the presence that troubled his existence uncoil itself from sleep. He felt it settle around his shoulders, its touch light and delicate at first, yet surely and steadily crushing him, squeezing any vestige of hope, trace of reason, from his brain.

He gave up on the idea of shaving himself and yielding to the lethargy enveloping his body, he fell into the cushioned arms of the armchair, his hand automatically reaching for the bottle on the floor beside his chair.

With his long years of alcohol and drug abuse he had been steadily depriving his mind of sanity, and slowly cocooning himself in a web of paranoia.

He jumped at the slightest shadow on the wall, suspicious of everyone he came into contact with, his fear growing and growing until it became an all consuming monster that would eventually devour him.

Deep down in the chasm of his mind, a tiny spark of intelligence still recognised the fact, but he was now powerless to help himself. Dim recollections came, of faces peering worriedly into his eyes hoping and wishing him well. They too were powerless to rescue him. Perhaps if he had called out, taken hold of many hands that had reached out to help him along the way.

He felt the hardness enter his heart and his mouth clamp shut at the very thought of asking for help. So was it pride that kept him in this state, perhaps, perhaps not. This thinking was getting too hard for him now. He put the bottle to his lips. The bottle was half empty. Oblivion was a bottle and a half away yet. It usually took two bottles before he felt the darkness closing in. Unthinking, he reached for the packet of cocaine in his pocket. No, I don't have to go to work today, it will only make me high, he thought to himself. Today I want to forget.

The warm dark blanket of oblivion slowly enveloped him in unconsciousness.

His brain stirred a little in the middle of the night and he reached for another drink. As his hand circled the floor, searching, a brief thought of clarity, an observation, flashed through his mind. When did I stop using a glass?

Revulsion shivered through him. He had always managed to convince himself that he wasn't an alcoholic, that he always drank from a glass. How absurd, he now thought, and how long had it been since he stopped using one? He couldn't answer.

This thought frightened him even more and he reached for the bottle.

'No, No, NO,' he shouted out, the empty space echoing back his words. 'I damn well, will, drink from a glass.' A desperate clutch at some semblance of normality.

He staggered to his feet and stumbled his way into the kitchen. By some miracle he found one clean glass at the back of the cupboard. Perhaps there was hope for him.

A faint whisper of a smile briefly touched his mind, but never quite made it as far as his mouth, which remained in its usual gloomy melancholy expression. He saw himself reflected in the dusty shaving mirror on the window ledge, a remnant from the life of his father, who even when the new bathroom had been put in had still shaved himself here in the kitchen, to the annoyance of his mother. Mind you, she was eternally annoyed. He had enjoyed the silence, for a while, anyway, when they had both passed away. Who would have thought they would die so close together, his father first, and she a few months later. You would have thought she would have been happy not to be eternally annoyed any more.

He took the glass back to the sitting room and slumped into his usual position on the battered beer stained couch and poured himself a large drink. He drank.

Time passed in a dim haze. He came to with a shiver, his movement disturbing the shadows that had settled in the darkness. He felt uneasy. He ran his fingers through his hair, and scratched at his chin, feeling the stubble, he had given up shaving himself for two weeks now. He had never let himself get this bad before, he had managed to keep up some level of appearance, until the last few weeks at least.

'What the fuck?' he said to himself. 'What shite is passing through my mind tonight?'

Some dark whisper of light was trying to penetrate his brain. He recognised it from the time he had first started drinking. It had been absent for years now and he thought he had silenced it forever.

'It's too late,' he whispered quietly. 'There's no hope for the likes of me.'

In the bleariness of his whiskey soaked mind, he travelled back down the corridors of time, memories, glimpses, snatches of what seemed like centuries flowed.

'No, by God,' he shouted and reached for the bottle. In slow motion the bottle slipped from his grasp and fell to the floor, breaking into smithereens. The precious liquid escaped, slipping through the cracks in the floor. He staggered to his feet, blood rushing to his head making him dizzy. His right foot landed on the broken glass, sending pain shooting up his leg, making him lose balance. The corner of the drinks cabinet connected with his head on his way to the floor, causing him to lose consciousness.

A door opened in his mind. He stood trembling on the threshold. Light streamed forth from the open doorway. He so longed to step into the light, he had lived too long in the darkness. He heard the voice of his mother screaming at his father that his years of drinking had helped to smother.

'You are no good you will never amount to anything. You're useless, I am sorry I ever married you.' The phrase repeated itself, over and over, followed by the next mouthful of spiteful diarrhoea now vomited out in his direction:

'As for you, you big useless lump, just like your father. I wish you were dead.'

The voice softened, yet whispered darkly in his mind.

'You can't go in there, that's too good for the likes of you.'

The darkness took him for the last time.

Rosaline Murphy

The Vessel

Century
After century passes
As the vessel sails the Sea of Reason
Seeking a shore on which to land.
Battered by harsh winds of condemnation,
Frozen by the bitter winds of icy judgement,
Becalmed on windless waters from which all
Evidence of life had long since fled. Life that
Could not exist under the reign of Reason.

Reason that
Scorned hope,
Mocked faith,
Laughed at belief.

In the midst of storms, the vessel clings to hope.
Adrift on lifeless seas and windless oceans.
Songs are sung, songs of faithful expectation,
And faith and hope do not disappoint.
Storms cease. Bright breezes blow.
Land Ahoy, the shout goes up.
The long sought shore is reached.
Spirits soar, joy abounds.
The vessel is
Home.

RÓISÍN SHEEHY

Finding Love
Morning Diary 1/6/2012
Sliabh Rua
Sliabh Rua (English Translation)
Murúch an Bhlascaoid/Blasket Selkie
Piso 2, Calle De Ladera, Vigo
aoife@notelly.com
Ham And Mustard Sandwich
Princesa
Compañero

Finding Love

We believe that Lir's daughter Fionnuala
swam the lakes of Éireann singing to her siblings
        in order to rid them of Aoife's curse.
The truth is, she was calling to him
and when she finally met him,
        that is, Saint Patrick,
his only focus was preaching Christianity!
Time caught up with Fionnuala and Patrick forgot the gospel.
        Her nine hundred year old body crumbled to dust.

Cohen took Lorca's poem, 'El Pequeno Vals Vienes'
and being Mr Direct wrote
        'I want you, I want you, I want you' in place of 'Te quiero'.
When Suzanne met him, the timing wasn't right.
Being seduced by the monastery, he fled
        where women were the least of his distractions!

Anne Frank was lucky to live in a cramped flat
with Peter, the fella she liked.
        It was easy to put up with her nagging mother.
When they were escorted to Auschwitz,
love blossomed and death was a long moment.

The storm heaved over Poland,
there was no room for toxic gas.

Air was sweet.

Morning Diary 1/6/2012

At 4.30 I count the few stars that remain visible in the overcast sky. I walk down to the prom in Tramore, passing the salmon coloured eyesore apartments, making my way to the dunes. The tide is high but I don't feel the spray. Pigeons call to each other, softly alerting the stillness of the unfamiliarity of night's silence. I imitate the sound responding to them. My voice soars in the surrounding habitat that is free of humanity. Seeing a shadow travelling beside me I'm shaken momentarily until I realise that I'm staring at the presence of my being. I walk with it until it disappears. Glimmers of dawn edge away the darkness.

Returning back from the dunes, surfers are braving the waves.

A man's behind is showing until he sees me in the distance and whips a towel around his pale body. Passing him, now clad in swimming togs, he looks at me self-consciously. The clouds break up, showing glimmers of orange light that spread above the potholed car park after sunrise.

The tide has come right in and the sea is splashing over the prom. Parked cars are dripping with salt water. Mid-way between the Iron Man and the shore I see two black and white shapes on the surface of the sea. On closer observation I witness seagulls. I pause wondering if they'll ever budge. Up Gallweys hill, I glance occasionally out to sea until they diminish out of view.

Back in the house my body takes to the cold temperature of the shower water as I had an urge to get wet in the sea. I leave home and make my way to Liz's house, who is to give me a lift to Dungarvan.

In the car she talks of an old friend Cáit Ní Chatháin from West Kerry. She pauses for a second before saying the place name of Cáit's village, 'Cill Mhic an Domhnaigh'.

She says 'coill' [k'əil] not 'kill' [e], exactly how they say it in the Waterford Ring Gaeltacht. The sound leads us astray and we end up in Baile Uí Dhuibh.

Sliabh Rua

Bhíos mealta ag d'ainm. Bhí orm bualadh leat agus siúl ar do chnoc ach nuair a bhaineas amach tú bhíos ró mhall. Thachtaigh trácht an bhóthair binneas d'ainm agus bhí scála do chnoic réabtha ag bús deataigh, monarcha laíon adhmadóireachta. D'fhág an bus mé ag sráid tithíochta a chlúdaigh do chosa. Leanais falla cloch tirim agus treoraíodh mé go dtí do ghlúine, a bhí lúbtha ag titim an sruthán. Chuas thar an fhalla ionas go luífainn ar do bholg. Bhí capall díomhaoin, traochta ag féachaint orm. B'ait léi an bhean fhánach ag taibhsiú na dúiche nuair a bhí sí ina searrach lán de theaspach agus fuadar uirthi le cosa in airde sna goirt fhairsinge. Leanas ar aghaidh ach thána ar theorainn, gairdín príobháideach agus madraí ag sceamhaíl.

Le sceimhle coiriúlachta i mbéal an duine ritheann sé liom go dtiocfadh feirmeoir i mo dhiaidh agus gunna ina ghlaic. Iompaím timpeall ort agus siúlaim ar imeall do chliabhraigh. Tá do scamhóga pollta ag pollaí leictreacha. Cloisim eininí ag canadh san aitinn atá ag gealadh le ruacht do dhúchais. Bainim amach mullach do chnoic, a Shliabh Rua, agus déanaim néal codladh i bhfochar do mhuiníl ag éisteacht le cogar do scéil. Nuair a dhúisím tá gránacht an mhonarchan laíon adhmadóireachta clúdaithe ag blaincéad ceoigh agus leac oighir scaipithe ar na bóithre ag bagairt ar threasthálaithe fanacht glan ó do chorp.

Róisín Sheehy

Sliabh Rua (English translation)

I was drawn by your name. I had to meet you and walk on your hill but when I found you it was too late. Road traffic choked the sweetness of your name and the shadow of your hill was destroyed by the bellowing smoke of a wood pulp plant. The bus left me at a housing street that covered your feet. I followed a dry stone wall which led me to your knees that were curved by the fall of the stream. I went over the wall in order to lie on your belly. An idle, tired horse looked at me. She thought it odd, the sight of a wanderer dreaming the landscape, when she was a foal galloping wild in the open habitat. I carried on but came to a border, a private garden with dogs barking.

With fear of crime being thick in the air it crosses my mind that a farmer might come after me with a gun in his hand. I turn around you and make my way to the edge of your chest. Your lungs are holed by ESB poles. Birds are singing in the gorse that is brightening with the redness of your complexion. I reach the summit of your hill, Sliabh Rua and doze off within the shelter of your neck listening to the whisper of your tale. On waking, the monstrosity of the wood pulp plant is hidden by a blanket of fog, and ice is scattered on the road foretelling trespassers to keep off your body.

Murúch an Bhlascaoid

Is é siúl an Bhlascaoid
Rince an choirp

Lúbann mo dhroim
Imlíne an chnoic
Luascaim timpeall ar an
gcaonach bog

Go sroichim Ceann Dubh
Mo bhéal dírithe ar an spéir
Agus mé neartaithe ag an aer

Chím an beithíoch
Ag snámh na dtonn
Gluaisim go cam leis an
bhfonn

An guardal ag glaoch ó
Phluais Scairt Phiarais
Do ghlór mar ghreim docht

Ní bhraithim uaigneach
Luite i mbaol
ar imeall na haille

Mo chraiceann sleamhain
Lán de ghainní
Deantar eití de mo chosa

Blasket Selkie

The Blasket walk
Is the dance of the body

My back folds shadowing
The outline of the hill
I'm rocking around soft moss

Until I reach Black Head
My mouth reaches for the sky
I'm strengthened by the air

Cattle are swimming
The waves, I move
crookedly with the sound

Hearing Storm Petrel call
From Piarais's Cove
Your sound a tight grip

I'm not lonesome
Lying in danger
At the edge of the cliff

My slippery skin
Covered in scales
Legs become fins

Snámhaim mo shaoirse
Le creimeadh taoide
Is mise Murúch an Bhlascaoid

Beannaigh dhom agus mé luite
Go meidhreach le mo chéile,
An Charraig Aonair.
Ag ligint mo scíth

I swim for my freedom
With the eroding tide
I'm Selkie the Blasket mermaid

Greet me and I'm lying
Merrily with my love
The lone rock
Resting

Piso 2, Calle De Ladera, Vigo

I lived in a romantic apartment slap bang in the old quarter of the city. It was previously owned by Salesiana monks, was a dancer's paradise with spacious wooden floors, a tiny terrace, high ceiling and a winding staircase. Art supplies, water canisters and peculiar ornamentation were stored in any given space. The apartment faced west and I would watch the evening sun flicker over the Cies Islands. Behind the terrace, facing the hill, I would divert around broken glass and make my way to cestería classes.

The faulty construction of the surroundings exposed remnants of an old village. The beautiful teacher, Xus from Lugo, showed me how to weave bamboo and create baskets. Peixeiras, women fish sellers, and the occasional male companion would babble away and sing in galego, in a gentle rhythm that matched the intricate ornamentation of the craft.

I was generally exhausted after spending a day around the local teenagers with my pigeon Spanish. Rosanna, who was born in Argentina would notice me yawning and repeatedly asked;

'¿Roshina, estuviste botellón?'

This would get a good laugh out of the gang who assumed I was drinking and causing riot at the square until dawn.

Sometimes at night, the traffic noise, junkies shouting and the beep-beep from the pedestrian crossing would weigh on the loneliness that I felt in this foreign city. It was soothing to watch clothes dry on the terraces that were scattered all over the barrio. When the sun shone construction dust and grime floated through the space in the front room of the apartment.

Strikes and protests were frequent events on the main road below me. On a particular day, cleaners were in protest over lack of pay and a fire flared up with flames reaching my window at the fourth floor. I had no communication with the neighbours who lived above and below me. The photographer who had a business on the ground floor had gone home, far away from the chaotic nature of the city. In no time the council workers called by and hosed the fire out.

aoife@notelly.com

My sister is hooked
My brother is hooked
Even my mother is hooked
And I was hooked too once upon a time

I was drugged by your useless entertainment
You made an addict of me at 6.30
Every evening
And under your command
I refused to eat dinner at the table

Your superficial chat, violence and sex
A cheap ecstasy trip
Kept us coming back to you
Your sad clients hungry for more

The nation watched the night show
With adults holding their
Teddy antique accessories
Looking human and raw

Nothing beautiful and true
Will linger in your world
The angry presenter tore apart
The bear's stitched scalp

And all I could see was white fluff
I had something to say
But the wolf next door cried
'Shut up, I can't hear the blasted thing!'

Aoife Ní Dhochartaigh passed away at 26
I wondered about the glorious monotony of her
Family home
Where the telly was only heard through
The neighbour's wall

Did you feel out of place amongst your peers?
As they spoke for decades over what they watched
Every evening
But really girl, you lived longer than most of us.

Ham and Mustard Sandwich

I hand Maild the docket, the first order of the day. It's time for her to move her fat arse and do a stroke of work. Reading the order she spits,

'I'm not doing that.'

Maild refuses to do anything beyond the sandwich board.

'What's the matter with you?' I cry.

My plea is no use and I'm certain this woman is really gone for the birds. I've been run off my feet all morning, loading and emptying the dishwasher, serving coffee and cake with a choice of custard, cream or ice cream to the shower of tourists that flocked the vicinity.

I smile and chat, pretending their visit is an absolute pleasure, while Lady Maild retains her fierce expression and chews hard boiled sweets. It's no wonder my shirt is drenched in a lather of sweat.

Two slices of pan are taken out and I slap on the mustard and the ham with a slither of fat hanging off it. As I make my way to the customer I glance at my docket and notice in perfect, legible writing:

Ham and Custard sandwich.

Princesa

Every morning I passed you
As I hurried to work while
You waited on it
You seemed too clean
To be associated with the fat whores
Who were bunched up under neon lights

On my return home
To the romantic high ceiling apartment
You were never there
The sky was on fire
It settled cascading
Over the Cies Islands
While peixeiras weaved baskets
With raw weathered hands

At the Escuela de Idiomas
We met in the corridor
Your Brazilian smile radiated your eyes
It dawned on me that we were so alike
We went to language class
Lived in the same area
We even looked alike but
You were beautiful

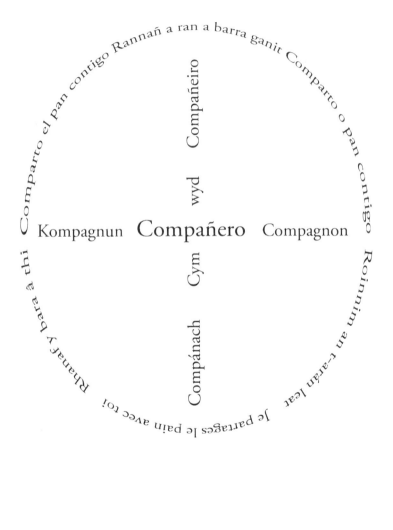

BILL WALSH

Alice Of Abervenny

My life's love was today torn out of me,
Laid in a shroud of Marram, raw with wounds,
The press of his last kiss; a memory,
In recompense; his three score killers bound,
Men covet glory but I know that whore!
She lures them to a brief sterile embrace;
The promise of shared joys behind, before:
A thirsty axe; cold comfort in its place,
Now, like the tempest drives a ship upon the reef,
I'll strike at any life within my reach,
With what honour would disdain, I'll purge my grief,
And raise a cairn of anguish on this beach,
Oh sated yet, you seagull choirs will be,
Till you cry out: 'Pity!' in polyphony.

Another Soldier's Song

(For Guardsman 8939)

Oh I could tell you stories boy
Of better men than me,
Of hardships shared and simple joys
And battles fought in Picardy.

I pulled men from a cave-in
When their gunners found our range,
I saw men wrestling with the gas
And, helpless, gulped in guilty air.

Three nights up on the Broembeek
In a shell-hole, rationing out black bread:
The look upon their faces
When we crawled back from the dead.

There's nothing like the taste of eggs
Fried on a trenching spade,
There's no Sacrament of God or man
Like friendships forged in mortal shade.

The boredom and the barrage,
Familiar echoes o'er the mud:
The high-arching whining mortar,
The shrapnel's stomach-churning thud.

Then the deafening sudden silence.
We prepared for the attack:
Fixed bayonets on the firing step,
'Steady; if they come on we'll have to drive them back.'

And we waited… like the prisoner
Waits the hangman's time to come.
Then the Captain said: 'Stand easy men,
Thank Christ our bloody work is done!'

We joined for flag and Redmond,
For bread and worth denied,
And many lived to tell a tale.
To whom? The turning world had died.

You'll never hear my stories boy,
My war was fought for you,
While I huddled in the Flanders mud,
You coughed your short life out to flu.

No stories of your war you'll tell:
A brave forgotten one,
Your Death Cert; coldly, proudly, reads:
You were a soldier's son.

In your mother's eyes a wound won't heal,
It drives a bayonet into me,
A no man's land in every heart
Is this war's legacy.

So in this old tin box, from the sight of day
I'll hide my hard-won medals,
The marks of loss and guilt and pride
In sadly equal measures.

But often in the dead of night
I wake up in a sweat:
Something's out there past the wire,
The gas is creeping towards us yet.

Do you smell it, do you see it?
No; this watch is mine alone,
And each comrade's lying wounded
In a shell-hole of his own.

I want to tell my story boy
Before this soldier fades away,
Like that good burning in your stomach
Of the grog to face the day.

And I'll drink to the man that knows me best,
I never learned his name,
I met him in a German trench,
We were brothers in this strangers' game.

Ball!

A distant silent puff;
Almost beautiful to see.

An iron ball comes bouncing;
Scythes a man below the knee,
And spinning on; a jet of red,
It leaves a hole, it takes a head,
The man beside me turns, I see
A question where his bowels should be,
Still smouldering and not content
Till all flesh and comradeship is rent,
Behind me, stifled screams confide
Imagined horrors magnified,
Where bone and bravery cannot,
Earth alone must halt this shot.

Self-buried in a bloody field,
Its wake of tortures unconcealed,
Only then its roar caught up,
Rejoicing in demonic work.

And among the furthest ranks of men,
That ugly puff begins again.

Ghosts

Of we who left before our time,
Our leaving, once was called a crime,
But in that desperate passage where we fled,
We found no solace with the dead.

Now, till dimly lit, the drinker drains
Rejected dregs, his thirst remains,
And yet, in earth must each his burden bear,
Lacking strength he had in air.

No. Early darkness brings no rest:
Our dismal sun is far from west.

And you, still quick, with empathy
For anguished souls you cannot see,
Consider, 'though you linger yet,
Perhaps your sun's already set.

Imprisoned, each within our time,
And law; to justify the crime!

If You Want To Be My Friend

There's a door and there's a cold wind blowing,
And I know how much you want to let me in,
This night is dark; there's only one star showing,
But there's a promise in that spark that night will end:

Don't let me in, don't let me in,
If you want to be my friend; don't let me in.

This fruit is sweet and God knows I'm hungry,
And the branch is offered low across the wall,
But if I taste, I know that greed will enter,
And the orchard will be open to the storm:

Don't let me in, don't let me in,
If you want to be my friend; don't let me in.

I'm carried on a river that will never reach the sea,
Across this cup of coffee your mercy's pouring into me,
And a wasteland that was barren is flowering like it's Spring,
I know you recognise me but
Can't you see the Hell that's beckoning?

Born of the same dust, parts of each other once,
In other lives we'll maybe meet again; who knows?
We must!
What's offered to us now is just:
A door, a star, a hunger without end.
No less; no more: If you want to be my friend,
If you just want to be my friend: Don't let me in.

Don't let me in, don't let me in,
Don't let me in, don't let me in.

Larksong

A Lark could sing that soaring wild and rare
I feel, when waking in your eyes I see,
Springing like cathedral vaults in prayer,
My own deepest love reflected back to me,
Not coldly, as in the mirror's hardened stare,
That barely grudges back an outward show,
But like some artist peeling layer from layer,
Unwrapping gifts bestowed above, below,
You fold me in your infinite embrace
That lifts me high above the realms of men,
Till love's far limits reached, our hearts condense,
Our souls, expanding, fill newer worlds again,
No words, no rhymes, befit such ecstasy,
But Larks hint at the joy that flies in me.

Saint Bridget's Day

As hard a winter as I ever passed,
I mourned good friends and lost friends buried me,
The blinds pulled down, sleet knocking at the glass,
No visitors; no comfort in my company,
Darkness carved a place to ponder here,
But reason holds no currency in Hell,
No insights born of misery and fear:
Guilt and innocence cohabit in this cell,
Woken by an urgency of wings
Flapping, panic-stricken, to be free:
A butterfly; transformed for better things,
The jailer and the jailed swapped clothes in me,
I raised the blind; I saw a life begin,
And through an opened window, light strayed in.

Sole Mates

Born, with every soul, there is a twin,
So through each life we search, sometimes in vain,
To reunite and close the void within,
For in that union, glimpsed, is Heaven's reign!
A creed for dreamers: We out-slept our day,
And woke into a world headlong towards night:
Each blindly grasping pleasure where he may,
In dread of dark; exalting meagre light.
How great my treason then, for I kept faith,
Till yearning racked my sinews from the bone,
I tasted bitter joy before its date,
And betrayed the task life set for me alone.
Forgive me Love: I did not wait for you,
And I've numbered with the damned, not one, but two.

Someone Else

There's someone else, she's just a friend,
I meet her every now and then,
Sometimes we talk, or not, but we don't need to;
She reads my very thoughts, my secrets,
And she just understands,
She knows my faults and only sees the better man,
I want to but I'm not seeing her.

There's someone else, she knows my name,
She calls me home from the world in pain
And heals me at her hands,
I can forget myself; she'll remember,
Resurrect me when I'm torn asunder,
I'll never know what she sees in me,
I'm a raging river to her sea,
God knows I want to, but I'm not seeing her.

There's someone else, I feel her near,
Tonight her perfume's on the air,
The room is hypnotised and staring,
Me: I couldn't tell you what she's wearing:
I only see her eyes; they smile for me,
She reminds me of the you that used to be,
And I'm not seeing her.

Spider

Oh Spider creeping 'cross the floor,
I didn't see you there before ………
Till I glimpsed you with a fright,
While seated on the loo at night.

Your many legs, your gigantic size
Completely took me by surprise,
What primal thoughts have you for me?
What compulsion urges me to flee?

How swift are you, the question begs,
Carried on so many legs?
Still faster I, I'll wager here,
Hastened by my phobic fear.

And rushing, frantic, to my bed,
A further visit I still dread,
Now, that I know 'twas not a dream,
Please excuse me while I scream!

AUTHOR BIOGRAPHIES

KATRIINA BENT

Katriina Bent is originally from Finland and has lived in the South-East of Ireland for almost 17 years. She was editor in an environmental weekly paper in Helsinki which gave her opportunities to travel and to write. While English is not her first language, her time in Ireland has deepened her love and understanding of it and enabled her to move from the factual to fiction. While she has worked in different fields, including people with disabilities, being a mother and the family is central to her life.

CECILIA CARELSE

Cecilia completed a science fiction novel 'The Alien Woman' last year, and has two other novels underway 'Things to Fear' and 'The 13th Vision'. She was awarded Artlinks Mentoring (2012, 2013), an Artlinks Bursary (2013) and a Regional Arts Bursary (2014) through the Arts Office, Waterford County Council. She completed a Cert. in Creative Writing for Publication (2012) and is on the Two Roads programme at NUI Maynooth (Kilkenny Campus). A background in engineering and photography, she has lived in England, Sudan, Nigeria, Zimbabwe, and over twenty-two years in Ireland. She enjoys hill walking.

GEORGE WILLIAM CURRAN

George was born and bred in Tramore, Co. Waterford and has been writing poetry for fourteen years, inspired by the timelessness of the poets Edgar Allan Poe, Byron, and Emily Dickinson. His interests are metaphysics, philosophy, bird watching, chess, palmistry, cycling, cooking, and music. He has worked in Holland, Germany, Israel, and Greece and now enjoys a quiet life.

BILLY FENTON

A glutton for punishment, Billy started writing a few years ago, instead of holding up bars throughout Ireland. And that was only his first mistake. Someday, he hopes to be published in the Dandy or some other serious publication. Once that happens he'll go back to the bar.

DARA FOLEY

Dara is a poet from Waterford who lives in Tramore. He loves to travel, surf and snowboard as often as possible. He draws inspiration largely from life experiences, nature, and time spent in Canada. His favourite writers are Leonard Cohen, Charles Bukowski, and Frank Herbert in no particular order. He also enjoys live music in all forms, and has a penchant for acoustic soul.

LYNDA GOUGH

Lynda has taken many years avoiding the place that gives her most pleasure. She now positions the pen over the page and has given herself permission to weave words.

ROSALINE MURPHY

Rose lives in Tramore and does as little as possible, apart from walking, sea swimming and writing. Her degrees are all self-bestowed and include living life at 180 degrees, and sometimes full circle. She's a master of all sorts, particularly expert on the liquorice. She has travelled far, moving home from one end of the Prom to the other and lives her life in tune with Popeye's motto: I am what I am. In other words, she is what she is.

RÓISÍN SHEEHY

Róisín's article, *An Corp Reoite*, based on her travels in Peru has been published in Feasta Magazine and her poem *Bá Eibhlín agus Dómhnaill* in Southword Journal's Summer Edition 2014. She is currently an apprentice writer on a scheme funded by Foras na Gaeilge. She has a degree in French and Spanish, and likes to express her creativity through dance and acting as well as writing. She's a wanderer and looks to the horizon.

BILL WALSH

Bill Walsh is a native of Waterford, where he works as a Chartered Architectural Technologist with a passionate interest in local history and conservation. His poetry often draws on historical themes at the human level where the common bond of deep felt emotion links us to the universal and the timeless. He sees dead people and communicates telepathically with cats. Do not approach him; he is dangerous.

EDITOR BIOGRAPHY

SUZANNE POWER

Suzanne Power has written novels, short stories, memoir, columns and poetry. Her work has been published internationally and has won awards. She teaches creative writing at NUI Maynooth, on a course she devised and founded, and in community settings. As an editor she has worked for many leading publications, with well known Irish writers and in editing anthologies she has helped writers to publication at all levels.

ABOUT WORD WEAVERS

Word Weavers is a creative writing group based in Tramore, County Waterford, Ireland. It was formed in September 2010 when the need for a second writing group in the area was raised. The group meets every two weeks and there's an open door policy to ensure that anyone who wants to write can join at any time of the year. They met in Tramore Library for the first three years and now meet at the Tramore Community Radio premises.

Facilitation of meetings is rotated amongst the writers every one to two meetings, and because of this they've tried out a diverse range of creative writing: poetry, short prose, short story, monologues, play writing, nonsense poetry and prose, location writing, aspects of the novel, characterisation, setting, dialogue, point of view, theme, as well as all manner of techniques to prompt new work. They hold the belief that every writer who facilitates has something new to teach the rest.

They want their members to believe in their writing voice and in themselves as writers. To remember that their writing is unique, perfectly formed, tumbling onto the page for the rest of the group to celebrate and embrace when it is read out loud. Like a pebble thrown up by the ocean's waves, the first raw drafts give the group a glimpse of the polished form to come.

This is Word Weavers' first anthology.